Coming Alive

What is Coming Alive?

Coming Alive is a ten-part course whose aim is simple –

- **to introduce you to the Person of Jesus Christ:**

  who He is, what He's done, why we can be so sure that He's alive today and how we can come to know Him for ourselves

- **to explain the basics of the Christian faith:**

  what Christians believe, why such faith matters and how it should be exercised and, in a word,

- **to help you to come alive:**

  in the discovery and deepening of a personal relationship with the Lord

How to use Coming Alive

The booklet can be used in a variety of different ways, and with people of varying ages and stages.

It can, of course, be used as a course for your own personal study; but it can also be worked through in the company of others, either on a one-to-one basis or in the setting of a small group.

Although you need read no more than the main text, which sets out and explains the essence of 'the good news', the booklet aims to make you think it through for yourself and (in the context of a group) to help you start talking about what you believe. Looking at the Bible passages given in the boxes and addressing the questions that follow is a first step to studying the Bible for yourself and seeing how its message all holds together – so although it may be tempting to skip these bits – try not to!

Welcome to Coming Alive

This ten part course falls into four main sections, as indicated alongside. It is intended to introduce you to Jesus Christ, and to help you reach a point of meaningful commitment to him.

One further booklet, **Staying Alive**, will help you take things further, beyond the point of that initial commitment.

Contents

The Membership Vows

When you feel that you wish to commit your life to the Lord Jesus Christ, that commitment is something that you are called on to make publicly.

Within the Church of Scotland that public profession of faith finds expression in the five vows listed alongside.

These are vows made before God, and it is important to have thought them through before we make them, since he takes them seriously, and expects us to do so also.

I believe in one God, Father, Son, and Holy Spirit; and I confess Jesus Christ as my Saviour and Lord.
This is the basic membership vow, which we will be exploring through parts 1 to 6 of the booklet.

I promise to join regularly with my fellow Christians in worship on the Lord's Day.
This vow begins to spell out the implications of our commitment, and we consider what it means in part 7.

I promise to be faithful in reading the Bible, and in prayer.
Part 8 tries to get to grips with what this vow means for us in our day by day lives.

I promise to give a fitting proportion of my time, talents and money for the Church's work in the world.
What lies behind this vow is worked through in part 9 of the booklet under the theme of 'Giving to the Lord'.

I promise, depending on the grace of God, to confess Christ before men, to serve him in my daily work, and to walk in his ways all the days of my life.
This final vow takes up the theme of discipleship and is covered in the final part of the booklet.

Good News!

In this introductory section we'll explore what lies at the heart of the Christian message – what it is that makes it both distinctive and attractive.

Often the problem that people have when it comes to the Christian faith lies in the fact that they start with a mistaken idea as to what the message ultimately is. The first task, therefore, is always to try and get clear in our minds what that message is – and what it is not! Only then can we begin to see what makes it truly Good News.

1 New Life

Here is the News

Familiar words for most of us – words that prepare us to hear what's been going on in the world in which we live. We like to keep in touch, we like to know what's going on, and so we listen in.

Often the news is bad, the events are sad, and the world seems mad! Death and disaster. Violence and vice. 'Wars and rumours of wars'.

It's a sorry picture painted daily on the canvas of contemporary history, and portrays a world in which we easily become discouraged, often become disillusioned, and are sometimes driven to despair.

But are we on the right 'wave-length'?

Here is the Good News

The Christian message is basically a 'news bulletin', an urgent announcement of something that has happened in the world we live in, an event that has repercussions for us all. God is at work!

The Gospel (or Good News) of Jesus Christ.

What makes the news 'good' is its offer of life: it is this, the enjoyment of new life, that lies at the heart of the Christian message, and at the heart of the Christian's experience.

A new life, where hope replaces despair, peace replaces turmoil, fulfilment replaces failure, and God replaces self on the throne of our hearts.

New life: abundant life: eternal life. But what is this life, and how can we know it?

What's going on in the world?
Write down the news stories that have hit the headlines in recent days and think about the sort of world they reflect.

What is the 'Good News'?
What, in a sentence or two, would you say is the Christian message?

A New Family

For most of us, our first contact with the Christian message will have been the church. How would you describe the church if someone asked you?

We tend automatically to think of 'the church' as a building, a place – and then, on reflection, realise that 'the church' is a people also: a people distinguished from other groups of people by certain noticeable features. Try listing some of these distinctives in the space below.

In a word, the church is a family – the family of God, the royal family, the family of the King of all kings!

The heart, then, of this new life lies in our being brought into a new family in which we come to know the Almighty God as our Father, in a very real, personal, and wonderful way.

Members of God's family
The church is essentially a group of people who believe distinctive things about Jesus, relate to God in a distinctive way, and live their lives in a distinctive fashion. They are a group of very different people, of all ages and stages, of all different gifts and person- alities, who in a real sense live out their lives together in the security of a common bond.

Read
John 14:6–8. Jesus is 'the life': here he helps his disciples see what it means to know him. Write down what he says is the great thing about knowing him.

Ephesians 2:11–19. Here are people who have been 'made alive' (v.5). Try putting in your own words what Paul says that has meant for them.

A New Person

. . . .

If you could change anything about yourself, what sort of things would you want to change? (You don't need to get too personal!)

The new life held out to us involves a significant change in our hearts and lives: it does not simply lie in our being brought into a new relationship with God, it lies too in our being made new people.

Most of us readily recognise that our problem lies not just in the fact that we've gone wrong (and as such need forgiveness), but in the fact that we go wrong (and as such need renewal); despite our best intentions, we never seem to get our act together and live as we should. We seem to have an inbuilt bias that sees our lives constantly leaving the straight and narrow.

The Good News offers the prospect of a new life whereby we are made new people: a new life whereby, deep down, in our very hearts, in the control room of our lives, a change is effected.

. . . .

Read
Jeremiah 31:33. God here promises that he will do something 'new' (v.31) in the lives of his people. Try putting in your own words what lies at the heart of this great promise and makes it so wonderful.

Luke 19:1–10. This story shows what Jesus came to do (v.10); in a sense, therefore, it helps us see what it's all about – an ordinary man being made a new person. What changes did Jesus make?

A New Start

However we think of it, this new life involves, of course, a new start. That, perhaps, is precisely what we want; it's certainly what we need.

We need to 'come alive'. But how? How do we become that new person and enter that new, royal, family?

Think for a moment about our own royal family. So far as we are all concerned, belonging to that family is just a dream (or a nightmare!), of course. The nearest any of us can get to the intimacy of the monarch's family home is the gates and railings of Buckingham Palace. We don't, and never will, belong, to that royal family.

But think of the ways in which a person does and can become part of the royal family (you won't need to think long!), and write them here:

When the Bible speaks about the way we become part of the royal family of God, it uses just those two basic pictures: it speaks of our being 'born' into the family, and of our being 'married' into it. And in both connections our attention is focussed on the person Jesus.

Jesus makes us new. This is the claim made about him. He is able to change our lives, able to effect such a radical change in our hearts that it is like being 'born' all over again – coming alive to God and his world for the first time: being born into his royal family.

Jesus offers us himself. He is set before us as the Son of God, the Crown Prince, who offers himself to us in love and friendship. As in marriage, when our lives are given over in response to him, then, through that relationship with him, we're part of the family! What he is, we are!

Everything, then, centres ultimately on Jesus: he can make us alive, he can make us belong, he can give us new life.

That's the claim that is made! That's the offer that is held out to us! It's a big claim; it's a marvellous offer! An offer we shouldn't refuse, and a person we can't ignore! What, then, are we to make of Jesus?

Read
John 3:1–16. Jesus uses a striking picture to show what has to happen if we are to 'enter the Kingdom of God' (v.5). What does he mean?

He also talks about having 'eternal life' (v.16): where does he say that the starting point for that lies?

Meet Jesus

· ·

Through this section we'll be trying to see just who
this Jesus is, and why we come to such startling
conclusions about him.

Is he merely one more entry in history's *Who's
Who*, just another great man amongst innumerable
such individuals – or is he significantly different?

Is he just an interesting, but remote figure from the
past, or does he have relevance for us today? Is he
long since dead and buried, or is he risen and
living?

And if he was so special a person, why did he die
such a sordid death?

The good news centres on a person: our next task,
therefore, is to meet Jesus.

· ·

2 Jesus: the Son of God

What do you make of Jesus? If you had to put your view of Jesus in a sentence or two, what would you say?

It's not an easy question! People have never found it an easy question, and all sorts of answers have been given.

But it's not a question we can ever escape, for in the end of the day we all have to come to a verdict about him.

'Who do you say I am?' asks Jesus.

Sometimes he's thought of as just a great teacher; sometimes he's thought of as just a great example, the ideal for us to emulate.

And yet, if he is merely that, he cannot really help us – and the message isn't really good news. Good advice, maybe; a good example, maybe; but hardly good news.

However, the Christian affirmation goes beyond either of those to declare that Jesus is uniquely God's Son.

What drove the first Christians to that staggering conclusion about this person? What drives men and women today to that same great conviction about Jesus?

We need to see that it is not wishful thinking that makes people say this about Jesus, but rather honest thinking: it comes from facing the facts about Jesus, and then reaching a conclusion about him that fits those facts.

What, then, are the facts?

. . . .

Read
Mark 3:20–22. Right from the start people found Jesus difficult to categorise! What do you think prompted his family to say he was mad?

And why do you think the teachers of the Law said he was bad?

Luke 9:18–20. Why do you think the people here came to these different conclusions about Jesus?

Fact 1

· ·

Jesus worked with unusual power

Whatever may have been the explanation there is no getting away from the fact that Jesus did some astonishing things.

He demonstrated a power over illness and disability, over demons and over death. He exercised a power over the 'forces of nature'; and in some ways most striking of all, he possessed the power to transform the moral and spiritual condition of men and women from all walks of life.

No wonder he attracted attention! No wonder he raised questions in the minds of the people who saw him.

How is this power to be explained? What explanations could you think of?

· ·

Read

Mark 4:35–41. From the start Jesus raised questions in people's minds: 'who is this?' the disciples asked each other (v.41). What do you think were the factors that prompted the question in their minds here?

And what answers might they have come up with?

Luke 7:18–23. John the Baptist wondered about Jesus as well. What do you think Jesus meant John to understand by the answer that he gave to his enquiry?

Fact 2

· ·

Read
Matthew 7:28,29. What do you think impressed the crowd when they listened to Jesus' teaching?

John 7:32–46. What was it about the teaching of Jesus here that made the guards say what they did (v.46)?

Jesus taught with great authority

Two things are very clear in this regard. First, when Jesus taught, people were impressed by the sheer authority which he displayed.

There was something about the way he spoke that made a deep impression on people, that gripped them in a way that was clearly different from the 'professionals' of his day. He had that indefinable 'something', which made him thoroughly distinctive.

But alongside that, people have always been impressed by the abiding relevance of his teaching also.

There was something, in other words, about the content of his message as well that was distinctive. It is just a remarkable fact that the teachings of Jesus have continued to have a relevance not only down through the generations, but right across the cultures of the world also, in a way that is true of no other teacher; the widespread, and long-term, relevance of his teaching is quite unique. He was clearly different: somehow we have to explain that difference in a way that fits the facts!

What's your impression of the teaching of Jesus?
· · · · · · · · · · · · · · · ·

Fact 3

· ·

Jesus lived with perfect purity

Three striking truths about the life of Jesus confront us. Firstly, he himself seems to have had no awareness of sin in his own life at all. For an individual of his moral stature this is quite without parallel, and argues either that he was hopelessly sold to sin, or that he was actually without sin.

Secondly, his friends were not aware of any sin in his life at all – and remember, they were with him, day in, day out, for months on end, seeing him in a whole range of circumstances, and under all sorts of pressure.

Finally, his enemies could pin nothing against him! This was one of the great problems that the authorities had when trying to get rid of Jesus.

Now think of yourself, your friends, and your enemies: it wouldn't be quite the same story! What might other people pin against you if they had the chance?

His life was quite unique! So what explanation will fit that fact?

· · · · · · · · · · · · · · · ·

Read
Luke 23:39–43. What do you think made the thief on the cross speak like this about Jesus?

John 8:46. What would you say is so startling about this challenge Jesus addresses to his opponents?

Hebrews 4:15. Write down what strikes you most about Jesus in this verse.

Fact 4

· ·

Jesus issued some amazing claims

Jesus made staggering claims! He claimed to be divine, to be eternal, to have the authority to forgive sins, to be God. There is little doubt that Jesus made these huge, and apparently blasphemous, claims – in the end of the day it was just because of these claims, sometimes implicit, sometimes explicit, that he was crucified.

We, like the people of his day, have to make some sense of the claims that he made. Think, for a moment, how you would react if someone in your street started making those sort of claims: what would you say about them? What could you say about them?

Ultimately, there are only three alternative conclusions open to us: we can say that Jesus was mad, that Jesus was bad, or we can say that Jesus is who he says he is.

The claims that he made thus drove the people of his day, as they drive us also, into a corner. We can't bring ourselves to say that he was mad or bad – that doesn't fit the facts! And that only leaves us the third alternative!

You must make your choice...

'A man who was merely a man and said the sort of things Jesus said would not be a great teacher. He would either be a lunatic – on a level with the man who says he is a poached egg – or else he would be the Devil of hell. You must make your choice. Either this man was, and is, the Son of God: or else a madman or something worse. You can shut him up for a fool, you can spit at him and kill him as a demon; or you can fall at his feet and call him Lord and God. But let us not come with any patronising nonsense about his being a great human teacher. He has not left that open to us. He did not intend to.'

C.S. Lewis, *Mere Christianity*. Read Mark 3:2–22 again!

· · · · · · · · · · · · · ·

For each passage write down what Jesus claims.

Mark 2:1–12

Matthew 26:62–66

John 5:1–18 (esp. vv.16–18)

Fact 5

. . . .

Jesus died and rose again

In some ways the most striking thing about Jesus was his death. Certainly the writers of the four gospels thought so, for these accounts of the life and ministry of Jesus all give a thoroughly disproportionate amount of space to the events culminating in and consequent on his death.

With a stark simplicity the record of his passion (suffering) reveals the nature of his person: the circumstances of his death provide the final credentials of his deity.

There was something quite unique, for instance, about the reason for his death. Why did the one person who never deserved it suffer such a terrible end?

There was something quite unique about the nature of his death. The land was enveloped in a terrible darkness and he was overwhelmed with a terrible desolation.

There was something quite unique about the **manner** of his death. Not the fact that he was crucified (that wasn't rare), so much as the fact that he embraced his suffering with a remarkable sense of purpose, endured it with a remarkable spirit of love and ended it with a remarkable statement of trust.

And there was something quite unique about the sequel to his death. Confirmed as dead, removed from the cross and buried in the tomb, he yet came back to life!

Jesus had died but was alive again!

His death is so remarkable and unique on all these counts that it can be explained only on the basis of the uniqueness of who he is – God's Son!

In the next two chapters, therefore, we'll turn to look more closely at his death and resurrection and see the implications for ourselves.

. . . .

3 Crucified Saviour

Everyone knows what the symbol, or 'logo', of the Christian church is – a cross.

It's simple, suggestive, and universally recognised; it's easily drawn, easily identified, and easily understood.

Just think, for a moment, how widely it's used as a symbol, and try listing below some of the very different contexts in which it's used:

It distinguishes a building as a Christian church; a book as Christian literature; a person as a Christian disciple – and so on.

We're perhaps so familiar with the symbol that we overlook how striking, and indeed how 'risky', it's first use actually was.

For the Roman world of the first centuries, the cross conjured up only one thought – the shameful and cruel death reserved for corrupt and criminal men.

Almost the reverse of its present impact! Like using a hangman's noose as the symbol of your message today. People would be struck by the sign, but not necessarily drawn to the message! So why do you think the early church used it?

From the start the disciples of Jesus proclaimed that the good news had its very heart in the death that Jesus died on the cross.

Their message was not just that this Jesus was the Son of God, that in a wonderful way God had come among them; nor was it just that Jesus was risen and alive; but that this Jesus, the very Son of God, risen and alive today, had accomplished something of untold significance in his death on the cross – something that had changed their lives and could change the lives of others also! Let's take a look, then, at that cross of Jesus and the death that he died.

Read

1 Corinthians 1:17,18 and 2:1–5. Paul clearly concentrated on the cross in his preaching. What one word would you use to sum up his reason for so doing?

Why did he die?

The story of the crucifixion of Jesus is well known, and most of us could probably state, at least in outline, what happened.

He was arrested: Where? By whom? Why?

He was tried: By whom? On what charges?

He was crucified: With whom? Why?

It's relatively easy to state the events leading up to his death – not quite so easy to give the reasons lieing behind it. But this much is clear:

He died unjustly

The most obvious truth about Jesus' death is that he was put to death unfairly at the hands of evil men. The Jewish and Roman authorities conspired together to get rid of him. Their reasons were various, their motives were mixed, but their desire was clear – Jesus had to go!

He died willingly

For all their scheming, the actions of these men didn't take Jesus by surprise. All through his ministry he had made it clear that his life would voluntarily be laid down, in accordance with the will and plan of God. The authorities were responsible for their evil actions, but God remained sovereign, and used their sin for good.

He died purposefully

Jesus had stressed all along that not only would he die, but that as the promised 'Saviour' he must die. Nothing less than his death would be able to accomplish the 'salvation' that had been promised throughout the Old Testament period by God. It was to bring that promise to fruition, and make it at last a reality, that Jesus died.

. . . .

Read
Luke 22:39–23:33. This is quite a long passage, but it's worth taking the time to read it, as it will help get clear in your mind what happened. Use it to fill in the details of Jesus' arrest, trial and crucifixion.

Acts 2:22–28. Why did he die? Peter's explanation here shows that there are different ways of looking at the question. What answer(s) does Peter give as to why Jesus died?

What does it mean?

. . . .

Read
1 John 4:7–11. What does John suggest the death of Jesus has to say to us? What are the lessons that he draws from it?

Different people see different things in the death of Jesus; but there are essentially three basic reasons why his death is so vitally important and significant, and we cannot afford to overlook any of them!

The death of Jesus shows us, first:

This is the way we're to live!
All through his life and ministry Jesus showed us life as it really should be lived, and made it so clear that truly to live is, in the end of the day, truly to love.

And in his death, more clearly and starkly than anywhere else, we see what that love essentially is: it is the willingness to give of ourselves for others, without limit and without condition – a love that has no bottom line.

If that were all, however, the 'news' of his cross would be anything but good! What a standard to live up to! What an example to copy! His cross would simply condemn us, and fill our hearts with a sense of failure.

But there's more!

The death of Jesus shows us, too:

This is the God we're to trust!
All through his life and ministry Jesus was also showing us God as he really is: we have so many mixed up and mistaken ideas about God which need to be, and at last are, corrected by our seeing the true picture in the life of Jesus his Son.

His death continues, and climaxes, that whole work of showing us what God is like, by demonstrating both the extent of his astonishing love, ready to endure such suffering for us, and the extent of his remarkable power, as he shows himself stronger even than death itself.

This, certainly, is good news! Yet even this doesn't take us right to the very heart of the significance of the cross of Jesus: we want ultimately not just to see God, but to know him. And by his death, we're told, Jesus has made that possible!

So, above all, the death of Jesus shows us that:

This is the price that's been paid!

We all readily recognise that 'No-one is perfect': we see it in others and we know it in ourselves. We all fall short, we all miss the mark of God's perfect standard. None of us measures up; we have wronged our Maker and our King.

Because he is the infinite God however, our wrong against him necessarily assumes infinite proportions! And therein lies our greatest and most pressing problem: for there is a price to be paid if our wrong is to be pardoned – an infinite price, quite beyond our capacity to pay.

It's that price that Jesus came to pay! Having lived the life of perfect obedience which we should have lived (but haven't, and can't!), he then died that terrible death of God–forsakenness which we should have died (but now needn't!).

The price of our pardon has been paid! Forgiveness for those who are rebels is now offered by the God who is righteous! Good news for all!

· · · · · · · · · · · · · · · · ·

Read
Isaiah 53:1–6 and 2 Corinthians 5:21. 'The essence of sin is man substituting himself for God, while the essence of salvation is God substituting himself for man' (J.R.W. Stott). What (if anything) do you find hard to understand in this?

How should I respond?

If forgiveness has become possible, how does it become personal? How does it become mine?

If Jesus has paid that price, am I 'automatically' forgiven, whether I realise it or not – indeed, whether I want it or not? Or do I have somehow to make it my own?

Does it matter, in other words, how I respond to Jesus?

The two passages referred to in the box on the right simply underline what the whole of Scripture makes quite clear – our response matters.

Like the thieves on the cross, each of us is either on one side or the other.

We're either for Jesus, or against him. We're either trusting him, or scorning him.

And, depending on that response, we're either with him (in heaven), or without him, and apart from him.

Forgiveness, then, is first of all required by us; but the 'Good News' goes on to declare that forgiveness has been procured for us, and is now offered to us.

God's forgiveness, however, needs finally to be received by us, through the exercise of a personal faith in Jesus, that Jesus who died, but is now risen and lives.

What that faith involves is the subject of the next section.

Read the words of this hymn through, in the light of all we've been thinking about in this section, and make them your own:

And can it be, that I should gain
An interest in the Saviour's
** blood?**
Died he for me, who caused his
** pain –**
For me, who him to death
** pursued?**
Amazing love! how can it be
That thou, my God, shouldst die
** for me?**

He left his Father's throne
** above –**
So free, so infinite his grace –
Emptied himself of all but love,
And bled for Adam's helpless
** race;**
'Tis mercy all, immense and
** free;**
For, O my God, it found out me!

No condemnation now I dread;
Jesus, and all in him, is mine!
Alive in him, my living Head,
And clothed in righteousness
** divine,**
Bold I approach the eternal
** throne,**
And claim the crown, through
** Christ my own.**

Charles Wesley
· · · · · · · · · · · · · · · · · ·

Why do you think that our response to what Jesus has done for us should matter so much?

Read
Luke 23:38–43. Jesus gave an astonishing promise in v.43 to one of the robbers; what prompted this great assurance?

Acts 2:36–42. Jesus is Lord! And forgiveness is possible! That was the thrust of Peter's message here. How did he say that the promise of forgiveness could become a reality for them?

4 Risen and Alive

You need to take a deep breath when you start reading the Bible and taking in what the writers are saying! Here you find not comfortable platitudes to lull you to sleep: here, rather, are stupendous assertions being made in connection with a certain carpenter from Nazareth, called Jesus.

Not only is this Jesus being described as 'the Son of God', he is spoken of as having come back from the dead and being alive today, as someone whom we, here and now, may meet and know. Son of God is one thing – risen and alive is another! The former may be interesting and unexpected – the latter is revolutionary!

And yet, this is the claim that Christians make, and this claim lies at the heart of the message. Jesus is not so much someone to whom we look back, as someone to whom we look up. It is not his memory so much as his company that Christians enjoy!

Most of us probably don't take easily to this claim when it is first put to us: it presents us with all sorts of problems, and we can come up with all sorts of objections. Try listing here some of the objections that you, or others, could readily raise to this claim that Jesus is risen and alive:

It's important, though, for us to realise that we are not being asked to 'take a leap in the dark', or abdicate our reason, when we're confronted with the claim that Jesus rose from the dead.

Indeed, there is actually a remarkable amount of powerful and compelling evidence – so much so that one High Court judge once said that 'no intelligent jury in the world could fail to bring in a verdict' in favour of this startling truth that Jesus rose from the dead; and a disbelieving lawyer, writing a book to disprove the resurrection once and for all, ended up convinced that Jesus had risen and was alive! (*Who Moved the Stone?* by Frank Morrison)

How can I be sure?

It was not only the first disciples, but men and women down through the centuries, who alike have been quite persuaded that Jesus is risen and alive. It's a conviction that rests neither on subjective experience nor on slender evidence.

It's a conviction, however startling, reached by facing facts and drawing conclusions. Let's look, then, at some of the facts, and the evidence they present.

Read
1 Corinthians 15:1–20. Paul commends the resurrection of Jesus to the Corinthians as an indisputable fact; what different types of evidence does he use here to prove his case?

Paul understood the resurrection of Jesus as being enormously significant; from what he says here, what hangs upon this central affirmation that Jesus rose from the dead?

1. The Empty Tomb

Jesus was crucified, and buried: of that there is no real doubt. Nor is there any doubt that a tomb in Jerusalem was empty.

The question is simply how that empty tomb in Jerusalem is to be explained in a way that fits all the facts. What possible explanations could you think of?

It was the wrong tomb! Yes, the tomb was empty – but it wasn't the tomb in which Jesus was buried! That would explain it, surely!

Well, it sounds good as a theory – but does it bear cross-examination? How does it square with the following facts, for instance:

The man who owned the tomb agrees not only that it's now empty, but also that this was the tomb in which Jesus was buried. He had taken the body of Jesus and buried it in his own tomb – he should know!

Some women carefully followed the burial party from the cross to the tomb, precisely because they wanted to get the right tomb for anointing the body of Jesus; and they're agreed that this is the tomb that's now empty!

Soldiers were posted at the tomb where Jesus was buried, and it is this tomb which is now empty.

. . . .

Someone took the body! Again, this sounds both simple, reasonable, and obvious. But actually it raises far more questions than it solves.

Try some detective work along these lines:

Who took (or could have taken) the body?

Why would they have taken it?

How could they have taken it?

. . . .

Jesus never died! This is sometimes known as 'the swoon theory', the argument that Jesus only seemed to have died on the cross, but recovered in the cool of the tomb.

Sounds good again – but it too has its problems! Try answering these questions that inevitably arise:

How did a weakened Jesus get out of the tomb?

How were his friends taken in by him?

How can the blood and water from his side be explained? (Read John 19:32–35)

Read
Luke 23:50–24:12. List the things about the tomb that made them wonder:

And so, we're left with this one explanation:

Jesus rose from the dead!

The answer Christians give may be the most surprising, but in the end it is also the simplest – and if indeed Jesus is the Son of God, it figures!

2. Eye Witness Accounts

One thing we simply can't get away from is the fact that there were people willing to affirm publicly that they saw Jesus, physically, in person, in the days after he had been crucified.

Here are some of the things that make this really very significant:

Their number runs into hundreds (1 Corinthians 15:6): this is not just the testimony of the odd, isolated individual, but rather the combined and consistent testimony of hundreds.

They are very varied people: they come from very different backgrounds, have very different personalities, and adopted originally very different attitudes towards Jesus.

They are shown elsewhere to be thoroughly reliable: at every other point, in other words, where their evidence can be checked out, they are found to be trustworthy.

They speak with total conviction: so persuaded are they of the truth of what they are saying that they are ready to die rather than deny it.

What explanations for this undeniable fact can you think of?

Maybe…

They were lying? It's possible, of course, but does it really fit the facts, or solve the problem? Why would they lie like this? Not least when it is so out of character for

them? And are people really prepared to die (and gladly) for something that they know deep down isn't true?

Deception as an explanation doesn't fit the facts!

. . . .

Or maybe…

They were hallucinating? This sounds fairer and more convincing – but even this suffers from grave defects. Basically the facts don't fit what's known about hallucinations!

These eye witnesses are very varied individuals (hallucinations happen only to a certain type of person), with no great expectations that Jesus would rise from the dead (hallucinations tend to be related to a person's expectations), who saw him only for a limited period (hallucinations tend to recur throughout life), and who on occasion all saw him together (for five hundred people to share the same hallucination at the same time is totally without parallel, almost more miraculous than the resurrection itself!).

Hallucination as an explanation just doesn't fit the facts either!

Read

Acts 1:1–8. Jesus says that his disciples are to be his witnesses. Later in this same chapter (v.22) it's made clear that they are to be witnesses to his having been raised from the dead.

Note down what the writer, Luke, points to as qualifying them so fully to bear this witness.

Again we're left with just one explanation:

They were telling the truth!

They saw Jesus risen from the dead! The Christian response is seen to be not the most problematic, but the only one that really fits the facts!

3. Changed Lives

. . . .

Read

Acts 3:1–16. If you'd been there as part of the crowd, what do you think are the things that would have struck you most?

Countless lives all across the world have been unmistakably changed for the good!

Sometimes there has been physical healing, sometimes there has been most noticeably a healing of certain relationships. But above all there has been a moral and spiritual change that has clearly transformed the whole of life in a wonderful way.

And each one tells very simply, but very sincerely, that it has been the living Jesus who changed them!

What we read of him doing, he's still doing! He is risen and alive!

. . . .

What does it all mean?

If it is indeed true that Jesus rose from the dead, and that he is alive and at work today, what are the implications for ourselves? Write down what it means to you, what makes it good news rather than just interesting information.

Now have a look at what the Bible says it means:

You can face Jesus with praise!

The resurrection of Jesus tells us something, first of all, about Jesus himself! It's clear now that Jesus can't be either ignored or doubted – the matter of who he is has been put beyond question: he is indeed the Son of God, the Lord and King of all, before whom the only fit response is to bow in glad worship and service!

Read Acts 2:32–36 and Romans 1:1–4.

You can face the future with hope!

The resurrection of Jesus showed that, in a world still full of injustice, God is in charge! It showed that he always has, and will have, the last word! We may be sure, then, that the day will come when all things will be put to right. God has given notice that not only is Jesus able here and now to begin putting our lives right, he will also return one day to put the world to right. He is the Judge, the One who establishes justice! Now's the time to get right with him!

Read Acts 10:39–42 and 17:24–31.

You can face God with peace!

We all know we've failed! The thought of facing a holy God and being called to account by him is not a comfortable one at all. But the good news holds out to us the possibility of forgiveness, by telling us that Jesus died to secure that forgiveness for us (see Part 3, Crucified Saviour). And his being raised from the dead reassures us that the price of that complete forgiveness has been paid in full!

Read Acts 10:43 and Romans 4:25.

You can face life with Jesus!

Because he's alive, it's possible for us to know him with us in our lives, day by day, person to person, just as truly and fully as those did who knew his physical presence right beside them. We may know him as our Friend, our Companion, the One with whom we share all things, and the One who shares all things with us. We may have a relationship with him in which we know him speaking to us, leading and directing us, reassuring and comforting us, protecting and enabling us – meeting us in our every need. 'What a Friend we have in Jesus!'

Read Matthew 28:16–20 and Luke 24:13–29.

You can face death with joy!

If his death and resurrection has implications for our past (his forgiveness) and for our present (his friendship), it also has great implications for our future! Death has been defeated! And Jesus shares that victory with all those who trust in him. So his resurrection is the guarantee that our bodies, too, shall one day be raised, and then, at last, we shall be like him, made whole and perfect, in both body and spirit. Death, for the Christian, is thus not the end – just the start of something much better!

Read John 11:17–44 (consider especially the implications of v.25), 1 Corinthians 15:19–23, 50–57 and 1 Thessalonians 4:13–18.

Knowing Jesus

In the previous section we were seeing that Jesus is for real. But we can't leave it at that, because the Bible insists also that Jesus is for you.

Whoever we are, we may have a wonderfully real, person-to-person relationship with the risen, living Son of God!

In this section we'll be exploring what that relationship is – how we enter that relationship with Jesus, and how we enjoy it as the most thrilling reality in our day by day lives.

And so, having met and become acquainted with him, we must go on now personally to know Jesus.

5 Faith in Jesus

Christianity is more a relationship than a religion! At the very heart of the message is a Person, the risen Lord Jesus Christ; and we are not only invited and encouraged, but called upon to enter a personal relationship with him.

Knowing about him isn't enough – we must come to know him, in a person-to-person way. But it's not easy relating to someone we can't actually see, and who was 'last seen' centuries ago! What are the problems that you, or others, might have in contemplating such a relationship?

The Bible is written to help us get to know Jesus personally; and from beginning to end it's made clear that the heart of that relationship with him is the exercise by us of 'faith'.

But what does 'faith in Jesus' mean? How do we enter that relationship with Jesus? It's to these questions that we must now turn.

. . . .

Read
Luke 23:39–43. Consider again the thief on the cross. What are the features of his response to Jesus that stand out for you?

John 20:30,31. When John talks here about 'believing' what does he have in mind? What is this 'faith' that issues in life?

Admitting your need

Unless we realise our need, we'll not ask for help. Unless we know our guilt, we'll never ask for forgiveness. And unless we see our sin, we'll not bother with a Saviour.

Faith starts, then, with an admission of our need before God — confessing to him that we've gone wrong, been wrong, and are wrong at heart. That admission of our need before God finds expression not just in our words (we say 'sorry' for what's been wrong), but in our lives (we stop doing what's been wrong). In other words, to use the language of the Bible, we must 'repent'.

Both Jesus and the apostles began their message with this call, first of all, to 'repent' — the call to acknowledge our wrong, and to make a break from it.

It wasn't always a popular message then, and it's not always that popular now! Why do you think we find it so hard thus to admit that need before the Lord, so hard to say sorry and to stop sinning?

Hard as it may be, this has to be our starting point. And perhaps the first thing we must do is simply to ask the Lord to show us just how much we need his forgiveness.

Erratum. The following should be in the box:
Read
Mark 1:14-20. Jesus' message was short, sharp and to the point! From the experience of the fishermen here, what would you say 'turning from your sins and believing the Good News' involves?
1 John 1:5-10. The view of many that sin either doesn't exist or doesn't matter is dismissed by John as nonsense! But what is sin? What does 'confessing our sins' mean?

Believing the truth about Jesus

While knowing about Jesus is never enough, it remains true that we can't get to know him without knowing about him, and becoming sure about him! And that takes time.

Relationships develop on the basis of what we know about another person: people don't usually marry the day after a 'blind date' after all! We take time to get to know another person.

And when God calls us to enter this relationship with Jesus he doesn't expect an immediate, 'blind' commitment of our lives to him. That would be unreasonable. But he does expect us to take (and make!) the time to get to know about this Jesus – as we've been doing – until we see the truth about Jesus for what it is: the truth!

What has helped you most to believe the truth about Jesus – who he is, what he's done, and why he matters?

Read
Romans 10:8–14. How do people come to believe the truth about Jesus?

Committing your life to Jesus

At the heart of any relationship there is commitment; indeed, we readily recognise that the depth of the relationship depends largely on the degree of commitment.

Think of any meaningful relationship that you have with another person, and consider whether there has not in fact been a degree of commitment exercised by you both. Almost certainly there will have been!

In marriage you see it most clearly of all; there, of course, the commitment is absolute, for the man and the woman commit themselves completely to one another in love – all that they are and have are gladly given to one another, in order that henceforth their lives may in the fullest sense be a shared life.

That perhaps helps us to understand what God calls us to in regard to Jesus: for when the Bible speaks about our exercising faith in Jesus, it sometimes uses the picture of a marriage relationship. He gives himself absolutely to us – and we give ourselves to his love, we entrust ourselves to his care, absolutely.

We hold nothing back, but say simply, 'Lord Jesus, I'm all yours!'

What keeps people from making this sort of commitment of their lives to him?

. . . .

Read
Luke 14:25–33. How do the two pictures Jesus uses (building a tower, and fighting a battle) help you to understand the sort of commitment he insists on?

Doing things his way

It's fine to speak about commitment! It's fine to talk of 'having and holding from this day forward, for better, for worse...' – but if that commitment doesn't find outward and practical expression, it's without real meaning, and is just a form of words. Parrots can produce words of commitment – but it's people not parrots that the Lord desires!

Think for a moment of any special relationship that you have with another person – maybe a particularly close friend, maybe your husband or wife. What are some of the ways in which your mutual commitment to one another finds expression?

Almost every picture that the Bible uses to help us understand the special relationship we are called to enter into with Jesus underlines that we commit ourselves not only to his care, but to his control as well.

He is the Shepherd of the sheep who loves us, but also leads us.

He is the Head of the body who supplies our needs, but also directs our movements.

He is the King of the kingdom who gives us his protection, but also his precepts.

Faith, then, means ultimately that I no longer do things 'my way', but seek now to do things his way. It means that I seek now to discover Jesus' will, and to do it, in my day by day living, and in my day by day relationships with others.

In that way, we are simply declaring to the world in the most clear-cut fashion the great truth that we have recognised and gladly embraced: Jesus is Lord!

. . . .

When you have reached the point of wanting to enter that personal relationship with the risen Lord Jesus, it's good to get on your own with him and make that commitment, person to person: admit your need, turn from your sin, and hand over your life to him.

You might find it helpful to pray this sort of prayer:

Lord Jesus, I admit that I need forgiveness: I have gone my own way, and have gone wrong in thought, word and deed. I am sorry for my sins, and want to turn from them to yourself.

I believe that in your love for me, you paid the price of those sins, and are able not only to forgive me but to change me.

I hand my life over to you, Jesus, as my Lord and Saviour. I put myself into your care and under your control. I will gladly live not just with you but for you, as you give me strength, all my days. Amen.

Read
1 Thessalonians 1:3–10. Here were people who had clearly exercised a genuine faith in Jesus: in what ways had that commitment to Jesus shown itself in their lives?

Matthew 7:21–23. There are two people in any relationship! We must know Jesus – but does he know us? What does he declare to be the vital element in our relationship with him?

What does he dismiss as inadequate?

6 The Holy Spirit

The Holy Spirit doesn't always get a 'good press'!

It's probably helpful to start by trying to see why our initial reaction can often be a rather negative one.

For one thing, the description 'holy' in itself can be enough to put us off immediately! For many people it can conjure up the idea of a 'holy huddle', something rather cold, austere and imposing.

Then, too, we can be uneasy because of the clear reference to a 'spirit' world – the more so when we read in the older translations of the Bible about the Holy Ghost! It can all sound rather spooky, and definitely not our scene at all!

When on top of that, we sometimes read of all sorts of strange and bizarre experiences and activities associated with the Holy Spirit, that can clinch it for us! And so, subtly, we can become subconsciously conditioned to say a quiet 'no thanks!' when it comes to any talk of the Spirit of God.

And yet, the Holy Spirit is integral to the 'Good News'! The message speaks not just of a theory to be accepted in our heads, but of a reality to be experienced in our hearts and lives. The Good News is a case not just of a new leaf being turned over (forgiveness), but of a new life being enjoyed – a wonderfully real personal relationship with the living Jesus.

The Holy Spirit brings that new life to our experience: the Holy Spirit makes Jesus real to our hearts, and helps us enjoy that ongoing relationship with him in our day by day lives. And the Holy Spirit enables us to know God as our Father in heaven.

We need to know about the Holy Spirit, and about the wonderful work of the Spirit in the lives of ordinary men and women like ourselves!

When people talk about 'the Holy Spirit' how do you react? Tick the word which best describes how you feel:

❐ Ignorant
❐ Confused
❐ Afraid
❐ Surprised
❐ Excited
❐ Encouraged
❐ Other (specify)

Why do you react like that?

Who or what is the Holy Spirit?

Read
John 14:16,17. Try and identify in your own words what different things Jesus tells us about the Spirit here.

Will the real Holy Spirit please stand up! Let's admit it! Most of us are slightly confused in this whole area! And much of that confusion probably stems from the fact that we often aren't sure how we are to think of the Holy Spirit.

Somehow the Holy Spirit doesn't quite fit into any of our 'animal, vegetable, or mineral' categories! Should we speak in terms of 'him' or 'it'? Is the Spirit some vague, impersonal 'Force' (along the lines of *Star Wars* for instance), or some distinct, personal Being?

How have you tended to think of the Holy Spirit?

The first thing we need to do, then, is to try and learn the right way of thinking of the Holy Spirit; and for this our starting point can usefully be the informal 'seminar' that Jesus gave his disciples the night before he was crucified. You'll find this in John 14–16.

The verses referred to in the box alongside (John 14:16,17) actually tell us a number of important things about the Holy Spirit.

The Holy Spirit is a Person
Not perhaps in the way we would usually think of a person, for the Spirit is neither physical nor visible – but a Person, and personal nonetheless.

Jesus speaks of 'another Comforter', indicating that the Spirit would fulfil that very personal ministry that Jesus himself had fulfilled.

He is the Spirit of Jesus
He is given by Jesus in order that we might know Jesus with us. In speaking of 'another Comforter' Jesus was really saying that although they would no longer have him physically with them, they would yet know him person-to-person with them by the Spirit living within them.

He is the Spirit of truth
In speaking of him in this way, Jesus suggests that not the least part of what he comes to do in our lives is to help us truly to know the one true God, by his both inspiring the writing of the truth of Scripture, and then also interpreting that truth to our hearts and minds.

What does the Holy Spirit do?

Does the Holy Spirit really make a difference? If we are confused about who he is, we can be equally confused as to what he does! And yet it is enormously important that we grasp the huge difference that he makes. God's promise, long before Jesus came into this world, was all along a new heart, not just a new start! He promised, that is, not just to forgive but to transform people. And the key to the fulfilling of that promise was to be the gift of his own Holy Spirit, the great 'Transformer'.

We've already begun to see (in John 14–16) something of what the Spirit comes to do; the verses in the box alongside fill it out a bit more. We could put it like this:

The Spirit brings the truth of God to our minds

He is spoken of as the Author of Scripture, the One who inspired men to write it, and now enables us to understand it. Through him we learn to recognise the voice of God, as he leads and directs us, as he warns and rebukes us, as he encourages and exhorts us.

He brings the love of God to our hearts

He enables us to know, not just in theory but as a great reality, God's love towards us as our Father in heaven.

He brings the character of God to our lives

He makes us like Jesus. We try (and generally fail!) to pull our socks up. The Spirit of God bit by bit gives us a completely new set of clothes!

He brings the power of God to our service

He equips us to serve the Lord Jesus, helping us to bear witness to who he is and what he has done. We couldn't (and wouldn't!) do it on our own, but he gives us the gifts, the courage, and the strength, to serve Jesus in the particular way that he has called us.

He brings the life of God to our experience

He makes us new people by coming to indwell us, and thereby breathing into us the very life of the eternal God. Not only, therefore, do we enjoy the throb and pulse of the life of the Creator God in our day by day lives here and now, but for the future we also have the sure hope that we shall share in the victory of the great Resurrecting God.

The Spirit of God doesn't simply make a difference to our lives – he brings a mighty revolution!

Read
Ezekiel 36:25–27. What is the thing that excites you most about this promise God makes?

Acts 1:8; Romans 5:5 and 8:9–16; 2 Corinthians 3:17,18; Galatians 5:16–26. From these verses try putting down some of the things that the Holy Spirit is said to do in the life of a Christian.

How can I know the Holy Spirit?

Will the Holy Spirit really 'work' for me? We need that revolution in our lives! But how does it happen?

Let's look, then, at how we can come to know his transforming work in our lives today.

We must, first of all…

Welcome him

Our lives must first of all be completely opened up to the Lord: we must welcome Jesus into our lives.

Jesus uses a very graphic picture to help us understand this. He makes it clear that all through our lives he has been knocking at the door of our hearts. He wants to come in!

Not only, however, does he want to come in, he promises that if we open the door of our lives to him he will come in, by his Spirit, to share our lives with us and to run our lives for us.

'I will come in.' This promise that Jesus makes to all who open their hearts to him is the starting point for our enjoying the work of his Spirit in our lives. But we need to go on from that to something further.

We must also…

Rely on him

When we welcome someone into our homes it makes a difference where we put them! And so, when we welcome Jesus into our lives, we mustn't put him in the 'box-room' (there if needed, but out of the way and largely forgotten) – we must have him in the 'control-room'! We must learn to rely upon him.

Remind yourself that he's there! We may not always feel different for having welcomed Jesus into our lives, but the fact is we are different – and that's what matters! Jesus dwells by his Spirit in all who have opened their hearts and lives to him. And just remembering that makes a difference:

> 'All God's giants have been weak men, who did great things for God because they reckoned on his being with them.'

They kept reminding themselves of this truth!

Ask him for his help! Jesus comes by his Spirit eager to share every part of the lives of his people with them. He is there to help! Indeed, there is no situation where he is not able to help us, as, equally, there is no situation where we don't need him to help.

Read
Revelation 3:14–22. Like a Porsche without an engine, the folk at Laodicea looked good, but were getting nowhere! They needed Jesus, and Jesus wanted in! In the same way, we, too, need Jesus – and he wants in to our lives also!

In what sort of ways do you think Jesus 'knocks' at the doors of our lives?

What keeps people from hearing him knocking?

What keeps people from welcoming him in?

Read
2 Timothy 1:6–14. Like Timothy we can often be very 'self-conscious'. Paul encourages him to think less about himself and what he is (and isn't!), and more about the Lord and what he gives. What does God give us by his Spirit dwelling within us?

But we do need to ask him! It may be to give us strength for a particular task, or guidance in a particular decision; it may be to resolve a particular problem, or to change a particular situation. Whatever it is, just ask him for his help and depend upon him to give it – always remembering that he is the One who

'by means of his power working in us is able to do so much more than we can ever ask for, or even think of' (Ephesians 3:20).

Finally, we must…

Obey him

Relationships are delicate things! Just as every human relationship can be tarnished by a lack of love, so something of the enjoyment of our relationship with Jesus by his Spirit can be lost by our disobedience, and the lack of love which that displays.

It's so very important, therefore, that in every area of our lives we learn to recognise what the Lord by his Spirit is saying to us, and to be ready to go where he calls us to go, to do what he calls us to do, and to say what he calls us to say. That affects our conduct, our relationships, our use of time – everything!

Not to respond to his promptings, not to obey his directions, is to be turning our backs not only on his Lordship, but also on his love – which inevitably affects our relationship with him.

He isn't gone, certainly, when we disobey and disregard him, but he is grieved; and we soon know the difference!

The opposite is just as true, of course! It's when we give the Holy Spirit full sway in our lives, when we're completely open to all that he is saying and doing, that our enjoyment of his presence and power and love is fullest also.

· · · · · · · · · · · · · · · ·

Read
Acts 5:17–32 (esp. v.32). In what ways did the Holy Spirit 'bear witness' in and through the experience of the followers of Jesus here?

Why do you think the Spirit was able to work so powerfully through them?

Follow Jesus

Making a commitment of our lives to Jesus is just a beginning! So often, however, it's just here that people stop short, failing to see that once we have entered into that relationship with Jesus we then need to work it out in our day by day lives!

The essence of that relationship, as we've seen, is expressed in the most basic Christian affirmation of all — Jesus is Lord! And that statement is not only declaring something about him, but saying something also about ourselves, and our relationship with him: it's an acknowledgement on our part that we're glad to have the One who runs the universe running our lives also!

But what does it mean for Jesus to be Lord in our lives? What will his running our lives involve? Those are the sort of questions that this final section explores, as we seek to understand what it means truly to follow Jesus.

7 Worship the Lord

Maybe it's the upbringing we've had in Presbyterian Scotland! Maybe it's the hang-ups we've got from a guilt-ridden conscience! But somewhere along the line we often seem to get the idea that if something's nice, it must also be naughty.

We take cream on our strawberries, but we know that we shouldn't. It pleases the taste buds, but ruins the diet sheets! It's nice, but it's naughty!

Subconsciously, we begin to assume that because the naughty often seems so nice, the things that are best for us are going to be a bind.

There are probably few places where this is more true than in worship. Engaging in worship hardly seems the most attractive proposition for large numbers of people: they know that they should, and it's meant to be good for them — but often they wish they didn't have to!

What would you say makes people think like this about worship?

Worship is meant to be a delight rather than a duty, a blessed reality in our daily lives rather than a boring ritual once a week! We're meant to enjoy it rather than endure it! But for that we need to see it for what it is.

. . . .

How have you tended to think of worship? Which of these words best describes your feelings about it?

- ❐ Boring
- ❐ Predictable
- ❐ Unintelligible
- ❐ Exciting
- ❐ Transforming
- ❐ Comforting
- ❐ Other (specify)

What makes you feel like that about it?

What is worship?

'Worship' conjures up all sorts of pictures in our minds, and those pictures all colour our feelings about it. Think for a moment of the picture that the word 'worship' prompts in your mind, even now as you read it. Then underline in the description below those parts that are similar to your own picture.

An old (and old-fashioned) building... rather gloomily lit (and often somewhat cold)... with a minister dressed in sombre black robes (which seem to date from the middle ages)... leading a congregation of largely elderly (and not always enthusiastic) folk... through a repertoire of poorly sung hymns dating from at least a century ago... interspersed with prayers, readings and an 'address', all in a style of English that went out with the dinosaurs (almost!).

If these are the sort of pictures that flash through our minds when we think of 'worship', then it's easy to see why we're not always so keen on it!

But are they the right pictures?

Let's consider, then, the three 'primary colours' that combine to make up the true picture of worship, and make it, properly understood, something lively, exciting and enriching – whether that's the worship of Christians together, or the worship of our daily lives.

Praise!

Worship really means 'worthship': it is essentially our expressing the conviction that the Lord is altogether worthy of our praise and our love, the giving of our lives to him, and the living of our lives for him.

The first of the 'primary colours' in worship is simply showing the Lord, in varied ways, how great we know him to be, and how glad we are to enthrone him.

In what ways can we do that?

Read

Luke 19:28–40. Here's a good working picture of what worship really is – welcoming Jesus as King.

What are the features of this welcome, and the worship expressed here, that particularly strike you?

Joy!

Worship involves getting our eyes on the Lord — seeing him for who he is, and thanking him for what he's done.

We celebrate One who has done, and continues to do, great things! We rejoice at all that the risen, living Jesus has done, and is doing (in our own day, and in our own lives). Lives have been changed, needs have been met!

Why do you think this note of joy is often sadly lacking in the lives and worship of so many people?

Expectancy!

Worship centres on the living God, and the welcome that we afford by opening our hearts and lives to him leaves the way open for this mighty King to accomplish yet more in and through our lives.

He is the Creator God, and the welcome that we afford him, the worship that we offer him, throb alike with the expectancy that he will do a new thing, and that anything may happen!

What helps create this expectancy in your heart? How do we become more expectant?

· · · · · · · · · · · · · · · · ·

· ·

Why bother with worship?

Worship is much more than going off to a church service on Sundays! But if we can see why it's important that we do share in the worship of God's people on a Sunday, it perhaps helps clarify why it matters so much that our whole lives, day by day, are characterised by worship.

Most of us live busy lives! Sunday's a good chance to sleep in, to catch up, and to ease off. Let's ask the question then – why bother with worship?!

Why do you go to church? What makes you give that a place in your busy diary?

In the Bible it's made clear that worship is worth bothering about! And when we ask why it matters so much, the answers we're given are along these lines:

To worship the Lord is truly to love God!
To open our hearts and to offer our lives, to the Lord in worship, is just the truest and most fitting response we can make to the perfect glory of God, whose power can't be measured, and whose love for us can't be fathomed.

Worshipping the Lord simply shows that we have seen him, and now can't help but love him, for who he really is.

What most stirs your heart to worship?

To worship the Lord is truly to enjoy God!
It's only as we open our hearts to the Lord, and give ourselves to him in worship, that we can truly know him and enjoy him. As we can't enjoy a swim without immersing ourselves in water, so we can't enjoy the Lord without immersing ourselves in worship.

It's for that reason that the Lord calls for our worship – not that it might be a 'bind', but rather for our truest and fullest blessing.

What do you find enriching in worship?

To worship the Lord is truly to show God!
If in our worship we are telling the Lord how worthy we know him to be, we are at the same time declaring his greatness to the people round about us. A life of worship is also a life of witness, sounding out to others as well as up to God.

To know God at all is to want others to know him too. And just because our worship must always reflect the glory of God, it provides also a window that enables others in some small way to see that glory of God.

Read
Psalm 145. Listen in to this man who's worshipping the Lord, and as you do so try to identify what different considerations make that worship so important and 'necessary' for him. Why does he bother with worship?

How do we worship?

Why make Sunday special?

By setting aside one day in the week, and making it a special day of worship, we are simply following our 'Maker's Instructions': God's 'Rules for Living' direct us to make this a priority in our diaries, not least to remind us that he is God the Creator, in whose 'image' we are made, the One who made the world and 'rested on the seventh day'.

For the Jews that meant always the Saturday, but early on the Christian Church began to make Sunday that special day, calling it 'the Lord's Day', as a testimony to the distinctive Good News that lies at the heart of Christian faith and experience: for it was on a Sunday that Jesus rose from the dead, and on a Sunday that the Spirit was given to the Church. Our worship on a Sunday is, therefore, both a celebration and a proclamation of these great truths.

We need always to think of worship in terms of a relationship, rather than in terms of a ritual; for that reason the Bible never sets out a programme for worship, it simply lays down certain principles, which we each need to apply in our own lives and worship. We all tend to have rather a narrow and limited view of worship, and few things enlarge our vision and enjoyment of the worship of God more than a grasp of these basic principles.

Think them through, and try to see what they will mean for you as you worship the Lord.

We worship the Lord with all that we've got

This is the first principle impressed upon us. The Lord is so great, and his love towards us so amazing that truly to worship him demands our all.

We worship him from the depths of our hearts, and to the limits of our voices.

We apply our minds and our very bodies to the worship of him.

We employ all our energies, exercise all our gifts, and offer all our resources.

He is altogether worthy — and thus we worship the Lord with all that we've got.

We worship the Lord all of our lives

Not just on a Sunday! And not just off and on! The worship of God is not tied to any set place, or any set time, but is rather to be the occupation of our whole lives.

Day by day, task by task, our whole lives combine to be a medley of praise offered to the Lord in worship.

That's not to say that Sunday doesn't have any particular significance, of course!

In setting aside this one day and giving ourselves in a special, undistracted way to the worship of the Lord, we affirm that every day is given to him in worship.

We worship the Lord with all of God's people

It's a mansion, not a monastery, to which Jesus has brought us, as he makes us part of God's family! And it's clear that God our Father takes special delight, and bestows special blessing, when his family join together in praise and worship.

Symphonies of praise, rather than just solos, are the delight of his heart!

And as all the varied gifts of the musicians are required and combined to produce the beauty of a symphony, so all the varied gifts of the worshipping people of God need to be combined to bring an offering of praise that matches the glorious splendour of the God to whom it is addressed.

And it's there, above all, in the harmony of lives united in worship, that his presence is most clearly felt, his love most intimately known, his power most strikingly released, and his own heart most deeply touched.

· · · · · · · · · · · · · · · · ·

Read
Romans 12:1–9. Paul speaks here about 'the true worship' we should offer (GNB). In what does that consist, according to what he says here?

Psalm 150. We need 'all living creatures', the full 'orchestra', adequately to praise the Lord! Why?

8 Time with the Lord

We really are pretty 'mixed up kids'! How else can the fact that the Bible is the world's 'least-read best-seller' be explained? And how else can we explain the fact that we both turn to prayer so instinctively, and yet neglect it so emphatically?

There seems to be a kind of spiritual 'Jekyll and Hyde' about us all!

Bibles are acquired by us, then ignored; we swear by the Bible, and yet are bored by the Bible.

Why do you think this is so? What puts people off when it comes to reading the Bible?

Why do you find it hard to get down to reading the Bible? (Maybe you don't!)

It's little different when it comes to prayer. Virtually everyone has 'prayed' at one time or another: an instinct within us, it seems, prompts us to look to a help beyond ourselves; and yet this very activity that we can engage in at times so instinctively, we're also so reluctant to engage in the rest of the time.

An instinctive turning to prayer, and yet an odd reluctance as well. What do you think explains this strange paradox?

Jesus deals with mixed up kids! Not the least part of the new life that Jesus gives to us involves our coming alive to reading the Bible and praying – or, more to the point, the Bible and prayer come alive to us.

For that to happen, though, we need to break out of our deep-rooted 'hang-ups' about them, and see them for what they are.

Why bother?

Time! Most of us find that there is just never enough time for all the things that we would like to do – and as a result our lives involve an endless series of decisions about priorities.

What good reasons, then, are there for ensuring that time with the Lord (in reading the Bible and prayer) is given a priority place in the already full agenda of our lives?

We follow Jesus' example

It's not for nothing we're told that Jesus grew: the baby born at Bethlehem grew into adulthood. And he provides the pattern for our growth.

He is (uniquely, of course) God's Son, and as such he is the model for our growth as children of God, our growing more and more to know, and enjoy, and serve God as our Father. Jesus grew, and we too must grow in our lives as God's children.

For Jesus, central to that growth was the disciplined study of the Bible and the rigorous exercise of prayer. It's striking to find that in the three most central, and difficult, areas of living, the key to 'getting it right' lay always for Jesus in reading the Bible and prayer.

Facing temptation, making decisions, serving God. The three crunch points in our Christian living. When we face temptation, can we resist it? When we make decisions, are they the right ones? When we serve God, do we reflect him?

For Jesus the answer lay in Bible study and prayer. It's the same for us!

We value Jesus' friendship

Jesus is not just the King whose majesty we worship, but the Friend whose company we enjoy!

As in every relationship, so in this very special friendship, communication is vital: we need to take time with the Lord, both to listen and to share. That, after all, is how the first disciples found their relationship with Jesus developing into such an enriching and wonderful friendship – they spent time with him, listening to him, sharing with him, learning from him, talking to him.

That, in essence, is what reading the Bible and praying are really all about. The Lord speaks to us through his living Word (the Bible), and in prayer we speak to him! What could be better!

. . . .

What 'priority rating' have you tended to give to reading the Bible and prayer?

- ❏ Urgent (virtually every day)
- ❏ Pending (if I have the time)
- ❏ Out (almost never!)

Read

Luke 4:1–13; Luke 6:12,13; Mark 1:35-39. These verses give some indication of the importance that Jesus attached to the Bible and prayer in his own life – and they also help us see something of the reason why. Try and identify the areas of human experience where Jesus found Bible study and prayer so valuable:

Acts 1:12–26. Right from the start Christians have made reading the Bible and prayer a priority. Why did they take the time to do so here?

How do I go about it?

For most of us our problems with Bible study and prayer are not so much the theory as the practice. We can see why, but aren't so sure how!

There aren't any easy answers to the problems that we find, no magic solution that removes all the difficulties!

There are, however, certain principles (rather than set rules), and certain guidelines (rather than neat formulae), which afford some help, both in regard to our reading the Bible and in regard to our praying.

It's to them that we'll look now.

Be respectful as well as familiar!

The One to whom you come is your Father, and your Friend, certainly – but he is also your Creator and your King!

It is his Word that you read – and therefore a word that is full not only of love but of authority, a word to be obeyed as well as to be enjoyed.

And it is his presence that you enter – and therefore prayer is as much a case of our bowing before his throne as it is of sitting on his knee!

Not one or the other, but both! Respect and familiarity together!

Apply your mind as well as relying on the Spirit!

Both in reading the Bible and in praying we always need the help of the Holy Spirit – we must never forget that!

Make sure, then, that you ask him for that help – his help in understanding what the Bible is declaring, and in hearing what the Lord is saying; his help in kindling your praise and thanks, and in directing your requests and problems to the Lord.

But work in co-operation with him! Work at getting some order into your Bible reading and prayer, and think through what you are reading and what you are saying!

What for you are the biggest problems with reading the Bible and praying? (You're in good company!)

Engage in them at set times as well as all the time!

Jesus did just that! He certainly was in constant 'two-way' communication with his Father through the busy-ness of each day, and yet set aside quality time to be on his own with his Father in prayer and Bible study, day by day.

Any time – yes! All the time – yes! But set times, too!

That must be our pattern also.

Make them shared activities as well as personal ones!

We are part of a family, sharing our family life, as well as our Father in heaven, with brothers and sisters. It's important for us, therefore, to be studying the Bible and praying not only on our own, but with God's people also, benefiting from the different gifts and insights that our fellow Christians bring.

As a congregation there are times set aside week by week (in addition to Sunday) for just this purpose: try and make these times a priority!

Be patient as well as expectant!

When you read the Bible expect God to speak! When you come in prayer expect God to hear! But don't despair if you don't always hear him, and if he doesn't always seem to answer!

Learning to recognise our Father's voice, to understand what it is that he's saying, and to speak our own hearts – these are all part of our growth as God's children (as they are a part of any child's growth), and they require both time and patience.

. . . .

9 Give to the Lord

There used to be a whole series of 'good news/bad news' jokes. Some were better than others of course, but their humour really hinged on the fact that the same piece of news can be seen in different ways.

Jesus is no joke, certainly, but the gospel affords something of the same contrast: 'Jesus is Lord!' is both 'good news' and 'bad news' – depending on how you view it.

And so we find that this 'Prince of Peace' can be very disturbing!

We ask him to forgive us – only to discover that he means not only to forgive us but to change us; and hardly has that begun to sink in than we learn that he means not only to change us but to use us as well! We've been 'saved' to serve!

When we commit ourselves to Jesus as Lord, and say (effectively) 'Jesus, I'm all yours!', we make ourselves totally available to him – perhaps little thinking that he might just take us at our word, and use us in his work! It can be a shock to the system to learn that that's exactly what he does!

Jesus has become ours: all that he is and has is ours! But we are his too! All that we are and have is now his – his because he gave it all to us in the first place, making us the people we are and giving us all that we have; and his, too, of course, because in owning his Lordship we give it all gladly back to him, entrusting our all to his care and to his control.

Because, then, we are his, we seek to use all that we are and have for him – to further his work, to extend his Kingdom, and to advance his reputation in the world. How that works out in practice is what we'll look at now.

· · · · · · · · · · · · · · · ·

What do you find difficult in the thought that Jesus means to take your life and use it in his service? Tick the appropriate box(es)

❐ I'm not really worthy to serve him.
    (I haven't any right to such an honour!)

❐ I'm not really able to serve him.
    (I don't have anything to contribute!)

❐ I'm not really willing to serve him.
    (I want to remain my own boss!)

Where on earth do I fit in?

Finding our part in the service of Jesus can be as difficult as doing a 1,000 piece jigsaw! Like the four corners in the jigsaw, it's relatively easy to see the part that some have to play (the minister, the organist, etc.); a range of other people in leadership roles are perhaps like the pieces with straight edges which form the framework of the jigsaw.

But most of us are more like the hundreds of ordinary bits in the middle of the jigsaw! What makes it so difficult to fit those bits together?

Here are two simple guidelines to help you find your place in the life of Christ's Church:

Each of us needs to be actively involved
Just as every piece of the jigsaw matters if the full picture is to be completed, so, if Jesus is to be seen today, every Christian must play their part! That means living out our lives in conjunction with our fellow Christians, as an integral part of a local congregation – not as spectators but as participants!

Our commitment to Christ, therefore, properly understood, is always inseparable from our 'joining the church'. To know God as our Father is to belong to his family; to have Christ as our 'Head' is to be part of his Body.

Each of us has been particularly gifted
Finding where you 'fit in' is a case really of identifying what your particular gifts are – yes! even you have been given a particular gift!

As in any body, every member has his/her part to play, some more obviously significant than others perhaps, but all important for the whole body to function effectively.

What each of us has to do then (and we need others to help us in this), is first to recognise what our particular gifts are, then to see where we can best utilise them within the life of the church, and finally to exercise those gifts in the service of Christ.

This is what Scripture has to say about 'gifts':

1. Spiritual gifts are given to all Christians (not just to some): all of us, in other words, have some gifts, while none of us has them all!

2. Spiritual gifts are given by Christ (rather than chosen by us): when we commit our lives to Jesus he gives each of us, by his Spirit within us and through his love for us, those gifts which he wants us to have and use.

3. Spiritual gifts are given for service (rather than for our own satisfaction); these gifts are to be used by us, together, for God's glory!

Try to identify where your gifts may lie. (Appendix 1, 'Where do I fit in?' might help.)

Read
1 Corinthians 12

vv.1–11. In these verses Paul establishes certain basic principles that apply in regard to the exercise of our 'spiritual gifts'. Try putting down in your own words the important lessons he is teaching.

vv.12–31. In what ways does his picture of the 'body' help you understand how we should give ourselves in the service of Jesus?

What on earth are we doing?

We all have a part to play, then, in serving the Lord – a part that we discover increasingly as we become actively involved in the life and work of the church.

We give to the Lord by constantly offering our resources, our time, our abilities, along with those of other Christians, and making them available for all that the risen Jesus is doing in and through his church.

But what is he doing? What is Jesus working to do in and through his church here on earth today? If we're to be part of that work we need to know what it is!

What is the church here for? Have you ever stopped to consider that? What has been your answer?

It's a big question, of course! But the sort of answer that the Bible gives to us is along these lines, stressing a 'three-dimensional' responsibility:

We have the task of offering praise to the Lord!

We have, first, a responsibility towards God, as 'the King's priests' (GNB).

Our first task is to offer up a sacrifice of praise – and it's a task that requires us all, combining our resources and our gifts and our time in a great crescendo of praise to affirm the greatness of our God and Father.

We have the task of offering love to our people!

We've been brought into a family (made 'his people' (GNB)), and we have a responsibility also, therefore, towards one another.

We have the task of so using our resources, time and gifts, that we give each other something of a foretaste of heaven, the family home of our Father, as together we create an environment of mutual love and encouragement.

We have the task of offering Christ to the world!

Good News is to be shared! God sent his Son into this world, and Jesus now sends us into the world.

We have a responsibility as well, therefore, towards the world, for we are called to 'proclaim the wonderful acts of God' (GNB). And that, too, is a task that involves us all, and all our varied resources.

. . . .

Read
1 Peter 2:9,10. Here's a brief description of the church which helps us see what our responsibility now is as followers of Jesus. From what Peter says here how would you describe that responsibility?

How on earth should I give?

When someone you love gives you something, what are the things about the gift, or the giving, that mean most to you? And why?

Almost invariably it's not so much what we give as what lies behind our giving that means most to us – the thought that's gone into it, the sacrifice that's been made for it, and so on.

That's as true in regard to our giving to the Lord as it is anywhere else. How we give matters as much to him as what we give. So let's take a look at some of the guidelines afforded to us for the giving of our time, our talents and our money.

We should aim to give proportionately

It's not the amount we give, so much as what that amount represents, which matters.

You find this 'guideline' in the Old Testament in the principle of 'the tithe' (giving a tenth of your income to the Lord – read, for instance, Leviticus 27:30–32), and the principle of proportional giving is certainly carried over into the New Testament. Luke 21:1–4 brings out the implications of this in a helpful and striking way.

We should aim to give sacrificially

No matter who we are, or what the gift, one of the things that makes any gift special is the sacrifice that's been made to give it. The sacrifice reflects our love, and it's that which means most of all.

You could read 1 Chronicles 21 to see this guideline finding expression in the life of David the king of Israel. Note his words, especially in v.24: 'I will not give as an offering to the Lord… something that costs me nothing.'

We should aim to give thankfully

Our giving is never with a view to our getting, but always in response to our having been given so much already by the Lord. The giving of our time, our talents, our resources, is always a thankoffering, whereby we express to the Lord our gratitude for all his goodness to us.

You'll find this guideline stated, for instance, in Romans 12:1 and 2 Corinthians 8:9

We should aim to give willingly

Maybe this is obvious! But it can easily be overlooked!

We give not because we have to (who really receives much pleasure from a gift grudgingly given after all? Certainly not the Lord!), but because we want to.

It's an offering (which we've thought through carefully and prayerfully, and which we present willingly) rather than a collection (extracted from us under pressure)! Read 2 Corinthians 9:7 to see this guideline stated.

Read
2 Corinthians 8:1–9:15. This is probably the best part of the Bible to turn to for a full and comprehensive set of instructions on the subject of giving to the Lord. Take the time to read it carefully, and then note down as many principles as you can in regard to our giving which you learn from the passage.

10 Discipleship

Read

Matthew 28:16–20. It's disciples that Jesus wants, not just 'converts': he looks for people who will follow him rather than just fill the pew. From what you read here, how would you describe the difference? What's involved in being a disciple of Jesus (rather than just a member of the church)?

'You pays your money and you takes your choice!' People like to think so, anyway, when it comes to Christian commitment!

Some choose the 'three events a life' level of commitment (what's sometimes spoken of as the 'hatches, matches and despatches' variety of church involvement). Some choose the 'two times a year' level of commitment (the Christmas and Easter variety of church involvement). Some choose the 'one day a week' level of commitment (the 'seen on Sunday' variety of church involvement).

All of them make the same two mistakes!

They assume that a choice is available, and that these are the options. In fact, both assumptions are wrong.

For one thing, Jesus doesn't offer a choice as to our level of commitment!

And, then, too, the commitment he calls for goes beyond any of the levels above!

Jesus calls us to an every-moment-of-the-day commitment to him, a commitment that's summed up in one word: discipleship. It's a big, nasty-looking word! What does it mean?

Jesus calls us, first of all, to be disciples

That means being learners: we are learning to obey all that he has commanded us. Like every learner driver, we make mistakes; but, like every learner driver also, we have our instructor right beside us, ensuring that those mistakes aren't fatal!

But Jesus calls us also to make disciples

That's not an opitonal extra for the 'enthusiasts', far less a job for the 'experts', but part and parcel of our being his followers. We can't be his disciples without being involved in making disciples. Life generates life! But how?

. . . .

Making disciples means speaking about Jesus

People can't know about Jesus unless and until they hear about him – and they can't hear about him unless and until someone speaks about him.

Which is where we fit in! 'You are my witnesses', Jesus said to his disciples, and with that he really gave us all the clearest 'job-description' we could have. Whatever else it involves, being a disciple of Jesus means speaking to others about him.

None of us finds that an easy thing to do, at least to start with – for all sorts of different reasons! But there are some useful lessons to be learnt by watching others in action, lessons which can help set us on the right road.

If you've ever served on a jury you'll know what it is to try and weigh up the evidence of different 'witnesses'. What are the features in the testimony of any witness that would make you inclined to believe him?

It's little different when it comes to the witness we give as disciples of Jesus. The story in John 9 (see box alongside) of the man speaking about Jesus and sharing him with others helps clarify certain important principles in regard to our telling others about him.

Be real!
The man spoke from first-hand experience: Jesus had changed him, and if he could say nothing else, at least he could stand and say that.

Be respectful!
The man wasn't pushy, but responded to the opportunities that arose quite naturally for him to speak about Jesus to others.

Be honest!
The man didn't pretend to know the answers to all the questions (and objections!) that were thrown at him.

Be bold!
The man didn't get a lot of support, but he had the great encouragement of knowing that at least Jesus himself would stand by him. You don't need more support than that!

. . . .

Help!
Most of us cringe a bit at the idea of sharing our faith, and talking about Jesus to others! What do you find difficult about it?

Read
John 9:1–38. This is a long passage, but worth reading as it tells the story of an ordinary, uneducated man speaking about Jesus to a range of different people. He is bearing witness, and what he is saying perhaps helps some of the bystanders, like a jury, to make their mind up about this Jesus.

Try thinking yourself into the situation as one of those bystanders, and note down what strikes you about this man's testimony, what you find compelling and attractive.

Making disciples means living for Jesus

Think for a moment of those who pointed you to Jesus and helped make him real to you: try and identify what it was about them that made the biggest impact on you.

Almost invariably it's how we live more than what we say that makes the most abiding and significant impression on other people. And thus it's never enough for us merely to say that Jesus is Lord, we must show it also by the way we live our lives.

If Jesus is Lord, it means, almost by definition, that he has come to be everything to us; we can say that easily enough to others, but we best show it by doing everything and anything for him.

As the song in the musical 'Oliver' has it: 'I'd do anything for you… for you mean everything to me.'

People need to see (as well as hear) that Jesus matters that much to us, that he means everything to us, if they are to see that he is, indeed, the Lord. That truth comes home to people, in other words, when they see that we do everything and anything for him. Whatever it is, then, that we may be doing day by day, whether paid or unpaid, whether at home or at work, whether responsible or routine, making disciples requires that we do it all for Jesus.

. . . .

Read

2 Corinthians 5:11–15. Here's a man seeking to 'persuade' others, a man who recognises the importance of not only his words about Jesus, but his work for Jesus also. He sees that how he lives is as important as what he says. What were the things that made him want to 'live only for' Jesus?

1 Thessalonians 2:1–12. In what ways did Paul's 'living only for Jesus' find expression here at Thessalonica?

Making disciples means submitting to Jesus

Very early the essence of the Christian message was packaged by the church in those three simple, but telling words – Jesus is Lord!

In a sense that said it all: the focus was personal and particular (Jesus, a Person not a philosophy, and this Person not any other), the message was compelling and relevant (is, not was!), and the claim was radical and revolutionary (Lord! – none less than God himself, the King!).

We began by seeing that the Good News has at its heart the offer of new life – and to know that life is, ultimately, just to know Jesus.

To experience this new life is really just to expose ourselves to his love, and that love towards us is enjoyed only as his Lordship over our lives is embraced.

And so, to commend his love involves commending his Lordship, showing by our full and glad obedience that 'the Lord is good!' It's only, therefore, as we live under his authority that we help others come under that authority as well.

Thus it is, finally, only by our being disciples (learning to 'obey all that [he has] commanded') that we actually make disciples!

This is the final joy and blessing in the gift of new life that God gives to us in Jesus – that new life is contagious! For we find that as we live the new life, we impart that new life to others. Coming alive ourselves, we're used to make others alive as well!

. . . .

If Jesus is to be known as Lord he must be shown to be Lord. And his complete authority is shown only by our complete obedience. Why do you think we are often so bad at that?

This challenge was once given by a Communist to a western Christian:

'The gospel is a much more powerful weapon for the renewal of society than is our Marxist philosophy, but all the same it is we who will finally beat you…. We Communists do not play with words…. How can anybody believe in the supreme value of this gospel if you do not practise it, if you do not spread it, if you sacrifice neither time nor money for it? We believe in our Communist message, and we are ready to sacrifice everything, even our life…. But you people are afraid to soil your hands.'

Is that fair?

How do you respond to that challenge?

Appendix 1
Where do I fit in?

Many of us are keen to be involved in the work of Christ's Church, but aren't sure where we fit in: we're not sure what our gifts are, where we're able to contribute, or how to find out! Two approaches to discovering where you fit in are listed below. Hopefully one or other, if not both, will help you!

In this first section simply put a tick in the appropriate box if you feel that the statement is in some sense 'you'.

Administration
❐ I have (even basic) secretarial skills

❐ I can happily do clerical work of one sort or another

❐ I am able to tackle financial matters

The Arts
❐ I play a musical instrument (specify)

❐ I would like to sing in a choir

❐ I can draw, make posters, etc.

❐ I enjoy doing drama

❐ I'm keen on 'craft', flower arranging etc.

❐ I enjoy writing

Pastoral
❐ I relate well to other people

❐ I'd like to open my home to other people

❐ I'm good at listening to other people

❐ I seem to be sensitive to other people's needs.

❐ I like to encourage other people

❐ I enjoy looking after babies and children

Practical
❐ I'm good at 'odd jobs' around the home

❐ I enjoy 'do it yourself' (specify particular areas)

❐ I like being 'in the kitchen'

❐ I don't mind cleaning work

Teaching/Evangelism
❐ I like explaining the Bible to others

❐ I'd really like to share my faith with others

❐ I seem to get lots of opportunities to speak about Jesus to other people

❐ I'm able to put things across to other people fairly simply

❐ I have a good imagination

In this section mark yourself out of 5 for each of the statements listed below (a mark of 4 or 5 will indicate it is one of your strong points, 0 or 1 will mean it is one of your very weak points). Write each mark in the appropriate box in the grid on the next page.

1 I am good at listening ☐

2 I enjoy explaining things to others from the Bible ☐

3 I love preaching/talking about Jesus to a congregation/group ☐

4 I am often used to bring others to faith in Christ ☐

5 I enjoy administrative work ☐

6 I feel a deep, caring love for those who are ill, and a call to help them get well ☐

7 I am handy at most things, and adaptable ☐

8   I am deeply concerned about the world and social affairs ☐

9   I am usually looked to for a lead ☐

10 I make helpful relationships with others easily ☐

11 Others are helped when I teach them things ☐

12 I love the study and work involved in preparing a message ☐

13 God has given me a great love for others, and a longing to win them for him ☐

14 I can organise well, clearly and efficiently ☐

15 Others find my presence soothing and healing ☐

16 I like helping other people ☐

17 I am active in service in the community ☐

18 In a group I am often elected chairman or leader ☐

19 I can encourage others and help bear burdens ☐

20 I love study and finding the facts ☐

21 My sermons/messages have been clearly blessed to others ☐

22 I find my life is full of opportunities to witness to Christ ☐

23 I love doing office work and doing it thoroughly ☐

24 I have sometimes laid hands on the sick, and they have been helped ☐

25 I am a practical type ☐

26 I'm very aware of the needs of society today, and feel called to do something about it ☐

27 When leading something I put a lot of preparation into it ☐

28 I really care about other people ☐

29 I have patience in helping others understand Christian things ☐

30 I feel a clear call to preach ☐

31 I love to talk to others about Jesus ☐

32 I am painstaking about details in organisation ☐

33 I spend time praying with and for sick people ☐

34 I spend a lot of time helping others in practical ways ☐

35 I feel God is at work in the world today and I must work along with him there ☐

36 I am good at delegating work to others in a team setting ☐

1	10	19	28	A
2	11	20	29	B
3	12	21	30	C
4	13	22	31	D
5	14	23	32	E
6	15	24	33	F
7	16	25	34	G
8	17	26	35	H
9	18	27	36	I

If your highest total is in row...

A your gift is probably Pastoral

B your gift is probably Teaching

C your gift is probably Preaching

D your gift is probably Evangelism

E your gift is probably Administration

F your gift is probably Healing

G your gift is probably Practical Help

H your gift is probably Service to society

I your gift is probably Leadership

Add up the totals along each line, and place them in the final column. By comparing the marks in the final column you may get some idea of where your sphere of service is likely to be.

Sometimes it's helpful to get a 'second opinion'! Try some of your closest friends, and see how they mark you against each of the statements, asking them to be as honest as possible. Don't let them know what mark you've put down!

These are only guides, but hopefully they will help you discover the gifts Jesus has given you, and where he means you to fit in!

· ·

Appendix 2
Baptism and Communion

The Church has always had two special 'rites' (called sacraments), given by God to help our insight into and understanding of the Good News, and at the same time to afford us encouragement and reassurance in our Christian lives.

Baptism is a once-for-all sign which marks our belonging to the Christian community; communion is a repeatedly enjoyed sign of our sharing fully in the life of God's family, through faith in his Son, Jesus. Both of them are God-given 'pictures' that appeal to all our senses, with a view to our both seeing, and being sure of, all the blessings God gives to us in Jesus.

Baptism

Baptism is essentially a 'badge of belonging': a slightly unusual 'badge' perhaps, but an identification 'badge' nonetheless!

It consists, very simply, of water being applied to us one way or another — either by water being sprinkled over our heads, or (as some branches of the Christian Church do it) by our bodies being immersed in water.

Baptism is not magic! To say that it is the badge of belonging is not to say that it makes us a Christian: for baptism doesn't do anything magically to the person baptised — just as a ring doesn't do anything to its wearer.

Rather, baptism is often spoken of as a 'sign' and 'seal' of the promise that God makes, and that's probably the most helpful way for you to think of it.

Baptism is a sign of God's promise in the sense that the water helps us see what it is that God is promising to us in Jesus: water being so basic to all life, it reminds us that God has promised us 'new life' in Jesus, a new life lived in the power of his Spirit and in the assurance of his forgiveness (his 'washing away' all that is and has been wrong in our lives).

In this sense baptism in water acts as a God-given 'visual aid', enabling us to see as well as hear the message declared to us in the Good News of Jesus.

Baptism is also the seal of God's promise, in the same way as an engagement ring or a wedding ring seals, or confirms, the promise made to a loved one. As the ring given is a lasting assurance in regard to the promise made, so God gives baptism to confirm to our hearts the promise he has made in Jesus. He means what he says — and he wants us to know and be sure of that!

We respond to that promise of God in faith (see part 5), but the reason why many are baptised as children is simply because God, who wants us to know him as Father through Jesus, all along dealt with people not only as individuals but as families, and included the children of those who trusted him in his promise as well. So, like a girl engaged to be married, baptised children belong to the Lord, but must still take him up on his promise themselves!

Communion

Communion began with the 'Last Supper', the meal Jesus shared with his disciples on the evening before he was crucified.

At that meal Jesus told his disciples that the bread he broke and then gave to them, along with the wine that he passed to them, were to be a reminder to them of him, a reminder that his body would be broken and his blood poured out, for them. Accordingly…

Communion helps us remember Jesus. Whenever they ate the bread and drank the wine, Jesus told his disciples that they were to remember him. Thus when we share in communion (or the Lord's Supper, as it is sometimes called) our minds and hearts are being focussed on Jesus.

Communion reminds us of his presence with us. As he was with the disciples, sharing that meal with them as their Friend, so he has promised always to be with those who trust him, sharing our lives with us.

Communion reminds us of his love for us. When Jesus broke the bread, he said, 'This, My body, for you', a simple but powerful reminder of that love which would see him give up his life on the cross for us. And thus, when we eat the bread and drink the wine we are being reminded in an equally compelling way that Jesus loves us, and in that love will ever give us his all.

Communion reminds us of his Spirit within us. At an earlier stage in his ministry Jesus had once said that he was 'the Bread of life': as we need our 'daily bread' for health and strength, and as without it we die, so we need Jesus truly to live – he alone can give us the strength we need for life.

So when we eat, or 'take in', the bread (a picture used by Jesus of himself) and the wine (a picture used by the Bible of his Holy Spirit), we are being reminded that having welcomed Jesus by faith into our hearts and lives, we now have him living within us by his Spirit to be our life and our strength.

Communion reminds us of his family around us. Jesus shared that meal with his 'friends' or 'brothers': and so as we share communion it reminds us that we're part of a huge family, both world-wide and forever – a family whom we are bound to love and to serve.

. . . .